EXPRESS NE

non-retirement guides

your savings

How to assess your savings, plan ahead and budget

Edited by Frances Kay

KOGAN
PAGE

First published in Great Britain in 2009 by Kogan Page Limited

Kogan Page Limited
120 Pentonville Road
London N1 9JN
United Kingdom
www.koganpage.com

© Kogan Page, 2009

British Library Cataloguing in Publication Data

A CIP record for this book is available from the British Library.

ISBN 978 0 7494 5588 0

Typeset by Jean Cussons Typesetting, Diss, Norfolk
Printed and bound in Great Britain by MPG Books Ltd, Bodmin, Cornwall

Contents

Introduction

If you are to get the best that life has to offer after retirement, it pays to make some effort in advance. Important events always require some preparation if we are to make the most of them. This book gives general advice to help you to sort out some of the practicalities involved. Its aim as a resource is to help you enjoy your retirement to the full.

The majority of people retiring today are fitter, more skilled and financially better off than previous generations. Also, thanks to improved lifestyles and medical advances, a great many of us can realistically look forward to 25 years or more of active life – 60 could be the new 30. As a result, planning for the future has become critically important. Key concerns are most likely to be money and what to do with your time. Other issues may well include where you live, how to keep healthy and how your retirement affects your nearest and dearest. This book shows what is possible, advises on the best sources of relevant information available and helps you avoid the pitfalls that can catch the unwary.

If you were to conduct a survey asking people approaching retirement what their major concern was, most people would say 'having enough money'. For some there may be no worries; they have planned the event for years, made maximum pension contributions, carefully invested their savings, covered themselves and their family in insurance policies and carefully worked out forecasting budgets. They may even have a 'to do list' of what they are going to spend their money on as soon as their new life begins.

For a large number of people, however, this is not the case. After years of giving minimal thought to their pension, they are overcome with anxiety and fear as they realise that soon they will no longer be drawing a regular salary. Despite having friends who are already retired and who seem to live perfectly well, they worry about not having enough to live on. Even quite wealthy individuals confess to conjuring up images of being cold and hungry. In most cases anticipation is far worse than reality. Retirement can be far rosier than many people imagine. As long as people are realistic, it is unlikely that drastic economies will have to be made. For many men and women who have only a rough idea as to their likely income and expenditure, the future may not be bleak at all. This book shows what is possible, advises on the best sources of relevant information available and helps you avoid the pitfalls that can catch the unwary.

1

Doing the sums

Those who profess total ignorance of their financial situation have no excuse. It is far more sensible to be a wise owl than a headless chicken. Doing some preparation, knowing the facts and figures, is the essential first step in your pre-retirement planning. To make a proper assessment, you need to draw up several lists:

- expected sources of income on retirement;

- essential outgoings;

- normal additional spending (such as holidays and other luxuries).

Second, have a think about these options under the following headings:

■ possible ways of boosting your retirement income;

■ spending now for saving later;

■ your wish list, if affordable.

Most difficult of all to compile is a third list of variables and unknowns. It is impossible to predict the future, but for those who wish to be prudent certain things should be taken into account in any long-term budget planning. The two most important items are tax and inflation. The findings of a recent survey suggest that a high percentage of those about to retire feel they have not made sufficient allowance for inflation. Others said the rise in energy prices meant that heating and fuel bills were far more expensive than they had anticipated. Additionally, there are other possible emergency situations, such as health. If there were problems, you might wish to make special provision. It is also impossible to predict how long you, your partner or any dependants are likely to live, so careful consideration needs to be taken.

When doing the sums, it helps to be realistic. Don't make the mistake of basing your calculations on current commitments and expenditure, because a number of your requirements are bound to change. The possible areas where savings can be made and extra outgoings need to be considered are discussed below. The most practical way of using the list is to tick off the items in each column that will definitely apply to you and, where possible, write down the expenditure involved in the adjacent box. Although this will be no more than a draft – obviously there will be gaps – the closer you are to retirement, the more sensible it is to do this exercise.

Possible savings

There's no doubt that going out to work costs money; it involves a fair number of expenses, not least travelling and clothes. When you leave your job, you will probably save quite a few pounds a week on average. Items for which you will no longer have to pay include: your travelling costs to and from work, bought lunches and special clothes, out-of-pocket incidentals. More good news is that you won't have to pay any more National Insurance contributions and, unless you choose to invest in a private plan, your pension payments will also cease. Additionally, when you retire, you will probably be in a lower tax bracket.

At the same time you may have reached the stage when your children are now independent, your mortgage is substantially paid off and you have stopped subscribing to a life assurance policy. One of the most enjoyable aspects of reaching state retirement age is that you become eligible for a variety of benefits. These include, for example, concessionary travel, free NHS prescriptions, cheaper theatre and cinema tickets (usually matinees), reduced entrance charges for exhibitions and a wide choice of special holiday offers. Some benefits apply to both men and women from age 60.

Another point worth mentioning is that many insurance companies give discounts to mature drivers. In some instances, discounts apply to those aged 50; other companies restrict eligibility to those aged 55 or even 60. Normally, but again this varies, the scheme is terminated when the policy-holder reaches 75. Most companies, but not all, extend the cover to a spouse or other named person with a good driving record. The discount for people over 50 ranges from 10 to

15 per cent. There are considerable extra savings for drivers with a five-year claim-free record. The best advice is to approach your existing insurance company first and ask what terms they will give you. Among those that offer special rates for mature drivers are: Zurich Insurance, Direct Line, Saga Services and Age Concern Insurance Services. It is also worth checking the internet, as a growing number of insurers give discounts to those buying a policy online.

Extra outgoings

There is no escaping the fact that when you retire some of your expenses will be heavier than at present. First you will probably be spending more time at home, so items such as heating and lighting are liable to increase.

If you received any perks with your job, such as a company car or health insurance, then unless you had a very generous employer these will have to come out of your own pocket in future. Equally, any business entertaining you enjoyed will largely cease, so no more free lunches. Entertaining will now have to be paid for out of the domestic housekeeping.

Another very important consideration is all that extra leisure. With more time available, you may be tempted to spend more on outings, your hobbies and on longer holidays from home. To avoid having to drastically retrench, these need to be budgeted for well in advance. Most people say that in an ideal world they would expect to be spending roughly double on entertainment of all kinds, compared with when they were working. Even voluntary activities have hidden expenses. For example, more use of the telephone, petrol costs, supporting fundraising occasions and so on.

Looking ahead, as you get older you may want more home comforts. Likewise, you may have to pay other people to do some of the jobs, such as the decorating, that you previously managed yourself. Anticipating such areas of additional expenditure is not being pessimistic. On the contrary, it is the surest way of avoiding future money worries. You may find, once you have sat down and worked out your retirement income in detail, that you are even pleasantly surprised.

Expected sources of income on retirement

Your list will include at least some of the following. Once you have added up the figures in the Budget Planner (Chapter 2, page 21), you will have to deduct income tax to arrive at the net spending amount available to you:

■ basic State Pension;

■ State Graduated Pension;

■ SERPS;

■ State Second Pension;

■ occupational pension;

■ personal pension;

■ stakeholder pension;

■ State benefits.

Additionally, you may receive income or a capital sum from some of the following:

■ company share option scheme;

■ sale of business or personal assets;

■ investments (stocks and shares, unit trusts, etc);

■ other existing income (from a trust, property, family business);

■ bank/building society savings;

■ interest from a National Savings & Investments bond or certificate;

■ endowment policy.

You might also be in receipt of income from an annuity. However, since at this stage you will be unlikely to have purchased one, this really belongs in the category of investment decisions.

Unavoidable outgoings

One person's priority is another person's luxury – and vice versa. For this reason, the divide between 'unavoidable outgoings' and 'normal additional expenditure' (see section following) is fraught with a certain amount of difficulty. Almost everyone will want to juggle some of the items between the two lists; or add their own particular commitments or special enthusiasms. What matters is the basic principle behind the exercise. If at some stage budgeting choices have to be made, decisions will be very much easier if you already know your total outgoings. This includes what you are spending on each item individually and those you variously rate as important or marginal.

Whatever your own essentials, some of the following items will certainly feature on your list of unavoidable expenses:

▦ food;

▦ rent or mortgage repayments;

▦ council tax;

▦ repair and maintenance costs;

▦ heating;

▦ lighting and other energy;

▦ telephone/mobile;

▦ postage (including Christmas cards);

- TV licence/Sky/digital subscriptions;

- household insurance;

- clothes;

- domestic cleaning products;

- laundry, cleaners' bills, shoe repairs;

- miscellaneous services, ie property maintenance, such as plumber, window cleaner;

- car, including licence, petrol, AA, RAC, servicing;

- other transport;

- regular savings and life assurance;

- HP/other loan repayments;

- outgoings on health.

Normal additional expenditure

This may well include:

- gifts;

- holidays;

- newspapers/books/CDs/DVDs

- computer expenses (including broadband);

- drink;

- cigarettes/tobacco;

- hairdressing;

- toiletries/cosmetics;

- entertainment (hobbies, outings, DVD purchase/rental, home entertaining, etc);

- miscellaneous subscriptions/membership fees;

- charitable donations;

- expenditure on pets;

- garden purchases;

- other.

Work out the figures against these lists. Then in order to compare your expenditure against likely income, jot them down on the Budget Planner.

Spending now for saving later

You may normally take the view that there is never a best time for spending money. But remember, retirement planning is different in that sooner or later you will need, or want, to make certain purchases. These could include paying off outstanding commitments, such as a mortgage. Most people's basic list – at least to think about – under this heading includes one or more of the following:

■ expenditure on their home;

■ the purchase of a car;

■ the termination of HP or other credit arrangements.

Additionally, there may be a number of general domestic or luxury items that you had been promising yourself you would buy for some time. The question is simply one of timing: that is, determining the right moment to buy. Typical examples might include a microwave, gardening equipment, a DVD recorder, a new computer, hobby mater-ials and so on. To help you decide whether a policy of 'spending now' is sensible, or possibly self-indulgent, there are two very simple questions you should ask:

■ Can I afford it more easily now or in the future?

■ By paying now rather than waiting, will I be saving money in the long run?

True, the issue may be complicated by tax and other consid-erations, but for most choices this very basic analysis helps greatly to clarify the financial arguments on both sides.

Home improvements. If you plan to stay where you are, the likelihood is that at some point you will want to make some changes or improvements. It is normally accepted that any significant expenditure on your home is best undertaken several years prior to retirement. As with many other important decisions, the question largely depends on individual circumstances. Some people find it easier, and more reassuring, to pay major household bills while they are still earning. Others specifically plan to use part of the lump sum from their pension to create a dream home.

To arrive at the answer that makes best financial sense, present commitments have to be weighed against likely future expenditure (together with what money you will have available). One important consideration is to make sure you know how long you intend to stay in your present home. Investing a fortune in a property and then moving a couple of years later isn't wise. Despite what people may think, it is rare to recoup all your expenditure on a property once you've modified it to your own taste.

Though it involves a few minutes' paperwork, a worthwhile exercise is to jot down your own personal list of pros and cons, under the headings: 'spending now' and 'spending later'. If still in doubt, waiting is normally the more prudent course.

Purchasing a car. There could be two good reasons for buying a new car ahead of your retirement. One is that you have a company car that you are about to lose. The other is that your existing vehicle is getting old and is beginning (or will probably soon start) to give you trouble. If either of these apply, then it probably makes sense to buy a replacement while you are still feeling relatively flush.

However, on the principle of 'look before you leap', company car owners should first check whether they might be entitled to purchase their present car on favourable terms. A number of employers are quite happy to allow this. Also, dreary though the suggestion sounds, if economies look like being the order of the day, two-car families might assess whether both are really as essential as before.

Paying off HP and similar. In general, this is a good idea since delay is unlikely to save you any money – and may in fact actually cost you more. The only precaution is to check the small print of your agreement, to ensure that there is no penalty for early repayment. A further exception to the rule could be your mortgage. An accountant could advise you; or, if you are thinking of moving (and the issue is really whether to transfer an existing mortgage – or possibly acquire a new one), include this among the points to raise with your solicitor.

If you become redundant

Much of the information in the earlier part of this section is equally valid whether you become redundant or retire in the normal way. However, there are several key points with regard to money that it could be to your advantage to check.

You may be entitled to statutory redundancy pay. Your employer is obliged to pay the legal minimum, which is calculated on your age, length of service and weekly pay. To qualify, you will need to have worked for the organisation for at least two years. The maximum weekly pay taken into account is £350 a week (this figure is revised annually, normally around February, to reflect any changes in the Retail Prices Index). For further information, see the Redundancy Help website: www.redundancyhelp.co.uk

Ex-gratia payments. Many employers are prepared to be more generous. HM Revenue & Customs (HMRC) allows individuals to receive up to £30,000 in redundancy pay/benefits free of tax, provided this is not one of the terms and conditions included in their contract of employment. Amounts over this are taxed under the PAYE system, so there could be an advantage in requesting that some of the payment be made into your pension scheme. For tax relief to apply, this must be done before your departure.

Benefits that are not part of your pay. Redundancy may mean the loss of several valuable benefits, such as a company car, life assurance, health insurance. Your employer may let you keep your car as part of your pay-off and might be willing to extend any health/other insurance cover for a few months after you leave. Some insurance companies allow preferential rates to individuals who were previously insured with them under a company scheme.

You could be owed back holiday entitlement for which you should be paid.

Your mortgage. Your mortgage lender should be notified as soon as possible and might agree to a more flexible repayment system. Check whether your mortgage package includes insurance against redundancy. If you have a very low income, you may be able to obtain income support (IS) to help with your mortgage costs. If your mortgage was taken out before 2 October 1995, IS would be obtainable after eight weeks. If it was taken out after 2 October 1995, you would normally have to wait for about nine months.

Other creditors/debts. Any creditors whom you may have difficulty in paying (electricity, gas, a bank overdraft) should be informed soonest in the hope of agreeing easier payment terms. There could be an argument for paying off credit card bills immediately, even if this means using some of your redundancy pay. People who have taken out insurance to cover debts in the event of unemployment no longer have the money taken into account in calculating their eligibility for income-related benefits, provided the money is actually used to pay off past debts. Previously, this only applied if the money was paid direct to a creditor, as opposed to being received by the individual.

Company pension. Company pension scheme members normally have several choices. This is dealt with in more detail further on.

Jobseeker's allowance (JSA). Even if you are hoping to get another job very soon, you should sign on without delay, since as well as the allowance itself (£60.50 a week) your National Insurance contributions will normally be credited to you. This is important to protect your State pension. To qualify for JSA you need to be under State pension age and must either have paid sufficient Class 1 contributions or have a low income. You must also be both available for and actively seeking work. For further information about jobseeker's allowance and other benefits, contact your local Jobcentre or Jobcentre Plus office. Or look on the Directgov website: www.direct.gov.uk

Redundancy helpline. Can answer queries on all aspects of redundancy. Tel: 0845 145 0004; website: www.redundancyhelp.co.uk

Money left unclaimed

Many people lose track of their financial assets, either because they have forgotten about them or because they do not know how to contact the relevant organisations that owe them money. If you think this could apply to you, the Unclaimed Assets Register might be able to help. The products they cover include: life policies, pensions, unit trusts and dividends. There is a small search fee, of £18, which is payable whether or not the search is successful. For further information, contact the **Unclaimed Assets Register**, PO Box 9501, Nottingham NG80 1WD. Tel: 0870 241 1713; e-mail: search@uar.co.uk; website: www.uar.co.uk

Both the **British Bankers' Association** (helpline: 020 7216 8909; website: www.bba.org.uk) and the **Building Societies Association** (T: 020 7520 5900; website: www.bsa.org.uk) provide free services to help individuals trace forgotten current and deposit accounts, and the **Pension Service** (T: 0845 600 2537; website: www.thepensionservice.gov.uk/tracing/) offers a similar service to help owners of old pension schemes trace their holdings. Also **National Savings & Investments** (Tel: 0845 964 5000; website: www.nsandi.com) has its own tracing service for lost bonds, certificates or accounts. For insurance policies, try the **Association of British Insurers** (Tel: 020 7600 3333; website: www.abi.org.uk).

There are plans, backed by MPs, for the Treasury to seize dormant assets and donate money towards good causes, including National Savings & Investments (NS&I) schemes. An account is deemed dormant when it has been left untouched for 15 years or more. With fixed-term accounts, the 15 years begins at the end of the fixed term. Cash ISAs will be included. Should you find a passbook for an old savings account long forgotten, take it to the relevant bank or building society. If your address has changed, you will need to take proof of your current address, such as a utility bill. If you can't remember the specific bank or building society, contact the **British Bankers' Association** or the **Building Societies Association** – see above. If you were to find account details while sorting out the paperwork of a deceased relative, you would need to take a copy of the statutory declaration or probate form when you claim the money.

Extra income

There are many State benefits and allowances available to give special help to people in need. Definition of need covers a very wide range and applies, among others, to problems connected with: health, housing, care of an elderly or disabled relative, as well as widowhood and problems encountered by the frail elderly who, for example, may require extra heating during the winter. Although many of these benefits are 'means-tested', in other words are only given to people whose income is below a certain level, some – such as disability living allowance – are not dependent on how poor, or how wealthy, you are. Moreover, even when 'means-testing' is a factor, for some of the benefits income levels are nothing like as low as many people imagine. Because this information is not widely enough known, many individuals – including in particular nearly a million pensioners – are not claiming help to which they are entitled and for which in many cases they have actually paid through their National Insurance contributions. A number of voluntary organisations also provide assistance to individuals, sometimes in cash and sometimes in the form of facilities, such as special equipment for disabled people.

For further advice and information, you could contact the following organisations:

Jobcentre Plus Office: Tel: 0800 055 6688; website: www.jobcentreplus.gov.uk.

Department for Work and Pensions: Richmond House, 79 Whitehall, London SW1A 2NS. Tel: 020 7210 3000; website: www.dwp.gov.uk.

Citizens Advice Bureau: 115–123 Pentonville Road, London N1 9LZ. Look under 'C' in your telephone directory or visit the website: www.citizensadvice.org.uk.

Age Concern: National Helpline, Tel: 0800 00 99 66; website: www.ageconcern.org.uk.

England, Astral House, 1268 London Road, London SW16 4ER. Tel: 020 8765 7200.

Northern Ireland, 3 Lower Crescent, Belfast BT7 1NR. Tel: 028 9024 5729.

Scotland, Causewayside House, 160 Causewayside, Edinburgh EH9 1PR. Tel: 0845 833 0200.

Cymru, Ty John Pathy, Units 13 and 14 Neptune Court, Vanguard Way, Cardiff CF24 5PJ. Tel: 029 2043 1555.

Useful reading

The Pensioners' Guide. An easy-to-read booklet that provides information about the range of government benefits and services for pensioners, obtainable from Jobcentre Plus or Social Security offices, Citizens Advice Bureaux and Post Offices. Also available in pdf downloadable format from the website www.housingcare.org.

Another excellent book, for those wanting detailed information about planning their finances, is *The Retirement Code* by Lyn Ashurst, published by Kogan Page, March 2009. The author is an authority in her field and gives a comprehensive and detailed study of a careful and planned approach to the retirement process, based on about 50 case studies. An interesting book that covers a lot of ground. For more information see Kogan Page's website: www.koganpage.com.

2

Budget Planner

It doesn't matter whether you're about to retire or are not planning to do so for several years, completing the following Budget Planner (even if there are a great many gaps) is well worth the effort.

If retirement is imminent, then doing the arithmetic in as much detail as possible will not only reassure you but also help you plan your future life with greater confidence. You'll feel better knowing how you stand financially. Don't forget that even at this stage there are probably a number of options open to you. By examining the figures written down it will highlight the areas of greatest flexibility. One tip, offered by one of the retirement magazines, is to start living on your retirement income some six months before you retire. Not only will you see if your budget estimates are broadly correct, but since most people err on the cautious side when they first retire, you will have the added bonus of all the extra money you will have saved.

If retirement is still some years ahead, there will be more unknowns and more opportunities. When assessing the figures, you should take account of your future earnings. Perhaps you should also consider what steps you might be able to take under the pension rules to maximise your pension fund. You could also consider whether you should be putting money aside now in a savings plan and/or making other investments. Imprecise as they will be, the Budget Planner estimates you have made in the various income/ expenditure columns should indicate whether, unless you take action now, you could be at risk of having to make serious adjustments in your standard of living later on. To be on the safe side, assume an increase in inflation. Everyone should, if they possibly can, budget for a nest egg. This is to help cover the cost of any emergencies or special events – perhaps a family wedding – that may come along.

Possible savings when you retire

Item	Est monthly savings
National Insurance contributions	....
Pension payments	....
Travel expenses to work	....
Bought lunches	....

Incidentals at work, eg drinks with
colleagues, collections for presents ....

Special work clothes ....

Concessionary travel ....

Free NHS prescriptions ....

Free eye tests ....

Mature drivers' insurance policy ....

Retired householders' insurance
policy ....

Life assurance payments and/or
possible endowment policy
premiums ....

Other ....

TOTAL ....

NB: You should also take into account reduced running costs if you move to a smaller home; any expenses for dependent children that may cease; plus other costs, such as mortgage payments, that may end around the time you retire. Also the fact that you may be in a lower tax bracket.

Possible extra outgoings when you retire

Item	*Est monthly cost*
Extra heating/lighting bills	....
Extra spending on hobbies and other entertainment	....
Replacement of company car	....
Private health care insurance	....
Longer, or more frequent, holidays	....
Life/permanent health insurance	....
Cost of substituting other perks, eg expense account lunches	....
Out-of-pocket expenses for voluntary work activity	....
Other	....
TOTAL	....

NB: Looking ahead, you will need to make provision for any extra home comforts you might want; and also, at some point, of having to pay other people to do some of the jobs that you normally manage yourself. If you intend to make regular donations to a charity or perhaps help with your grandchildren's education, these too should be included on the list. The same applies to any new private pension or savings plan that you might want to invest in to boost your long-term retirement income.

Expected sources of income on retirement

Many people have difficulty understanding the tax system, and you should certainly take professional advice if you are in any doubt at all. However, if you fill in the following list carefully, it should give you a pretty good idea of your income after retirement and enable you to make at least provisional plans.

Remember too that you may have one or two capital sums to invest, such as:

▧ the commuted lump sum from your pension;

▧ money from an endowment policy;

▧ gains from the sale of company shares (SAYE or other share option scheme);

▧ profits from the sale of your home or other asset;

▧ money from an inheritance.

A Income received before tax

Basic State Pension ....

State Graduated Pension ....

SERPS /State Second Pension ....

Occupational pension(s) ....

Stakeholder or personal pension ....

State benefits ....

Investments and savings plans paid
gross, eg gilts, National Savings ....

Possible rental income ....

Casual or other pre-tax earnings ....

Total ....

Less Personal tax allowance and
possibly also married
couple's allowance ....

Basic-rate tax ....

TOTAL A ....

B Income received after tax

Dividends (unit trusts, shares, etc)   ....

Bank deposit account   ....

Building society interest   ....

Annuity income   ....

Other (incl earnings subject
to PAYE)   ....

TOTAL B   ....

TOTAL A + TOTAL B   ....

Less higher-rate tax (if any)   ....

Plus Other tax-free receipts,
eg some State benefits, income
from a matured TESSA, PEP plan,
ISA   ....

Investment bond withdrawals, etc   ....

Other   ....

TOTAL NET INCOME   ....

Unavoidable outgoings

Item	*Est monthly cost*
Food	....
Rent or mortgage repayments	....
Council tax	....
Repair and maintenance costs	....
Heating	....
Lighting and other energy	....
Telephone/mobile	....
Postage (incl Christmas cards)	....
TV licence/Sky/digital subscription	....
Household insurance	....
Clothes	....
Laundry, cleaner's bills, shoe repair	....
Domestic cleaning products	....
Misc services, eg plumber, window cleaner	....

Car (incl licence, petrol, etc) ....

Other transport ....

Regular savings/life assurance ....

HP/other loan repayments ....

Outgoings on health ....

Other ....

TOTAL ....

NB: Before adding up the total, you should look at the 'Normal additional expenditure' list, as you may well want to juggle some of the items between the two.

Normal additional expenditure

Item   *Est monthly cost*

Gifts ....

Holidays ....

Newspapers/books/CDs/DVDs ....

Drink ....

Cigarettes/tobacco ....

Hairdressing ....

Toiletries/cosmetics ....

Entertainment (hobbies, outings,
home entertaining, etc) ....

Misc subscriptions/membership fees ....

Charitable donations ....

Expenditure on pets ....

Garden purchases ....

Other ....

TOTAL ....

NB: For some items, such as holidays and gifts, you may tend to think in annual expenditure terms. However, for the purpose of comparing monthly income versus outgoings, it is probably easier if you itemise all the expenditure in the same fashion. Also, if you need to save for a special event such as your holiday, it helps if you get into the habit of putting so much aside every month (or even weekly).

3

Pensions

Pensions are no longer providing the sums of money they used to. There are many people coming up to retirement whose pension schemes have been wound up and who have lost a large chunk of their savings. This is one of the most difficult situations to cope with. But despite this, next to your home, your pension is still probably your most valuable asset. It is therefore important to check where you stand – and what you can best do if damage limitation is required – to ensure that when you retire you receive the maximum benefit.

State pensions

You can get a pension if you are a man of 65 or a woman of

60, provided you have paid (or been credited with) sufficient National Insurance contributions. In time, the age of women will alter as the government has published plans to equalise State pension age for men and women at 65. This change is being phased in over 10 years, beginning in 2010. This will affect younger women only. Those born before 6 April 1950 have no need to alter their retirement plans.

Your right to a State pension

Your right to a State pension depends on your (or your spouse's) National Insurance contributions. Most people have to pay contributions into the National Insurance (NI) scheme while they are working. If you are an employee, your employer will have automatically deducted Class 1 contributions from your salary, provided your earnings were above a certain limit (2008/09 £105 a week). If you are self-employed, you will have been paying a flat-rate Class 2 contribution every week and possibly the earnings-related Class 4 contributions as well. You may also have paid Class 3 voluntary contributions at some point in your life in order to maintain your contributions record. If you are over pension age (65 for men and 60 for women) you do not pay NI contributions. There may have been times during your working life when you have not – either knowingly or unwittingly – paid NI contributions. If you have not paid sufficient NI contributions to qualify for a full-rate basic pension you may be entitled to a reduced rate of pension. However, your NI contributions record will have been maintained in the following circumstances:

If you have lived or worked outside Great Britain. If you have lived in Northern Ireland or the Isle of Man, any contributions paid there will count towards your pension. The same should also apply in most cases if you have lived or worked in an EU country or any country whose social security is linked to Britain's by a reciprocal arrangement. However, there have sometimes been problems with certain countries, so, if you have any doubts, you should enquire what your position is at your pension centre.

If you have received Home Responsibilities Protection (HRP). If you have not worked regularly at some time since 1978, because you have had to stay at home to care for either a child or a sick or elderly person, you may have protected your right to a pension by claiming HRP. This benefit allows you to deduct the years when you were required to give up work from the normal qualifying period for a basic pension and so, in effect, shorten the number of years when you would otherwise have been required to make contributions.

There are two important points to note. First, if you are a woman and were claiming child benefit, HRP should have been credited to you automatically, whereas a man staying at home to care for a child would have needed to arrange the transfer of child benefit to himself. Second, HRP is only available for complete tax years in which earnings were less than 52 times the lower earnings limit.

Although HRP can be claimed by both sexes, it predictably applies more frequently to women. For more information, see 'Pensions for women' on page 94 or obtain leaflet CF411, *How to Protect your State Pension if you are Looking After Someone at Home*, available from your pension centre. Or see website: www.thepensionservice.gov.uk.

If you have been in any of the following situations, you will have been credited with contributions (instead of having to pay them):

▦ if you were sick or unemployed (provided you sent in sick notes to your social security office, signed on at the unemployment benefit office or were in receipt of jobseeker's allowance);

▦ if you were a man aged 60–64 and not working;

▦ if you were entitled to maternity allowance, invalid care allowance or unemployability supplement;

▦ if you were taking an approved course of training;

▦ if you had left education but had not yet started working;

▦ if since April 2000 your earnings have fallen between what are known as the lower earnings limit and the primary threshold, ie (2008/09) between £90 and £105 a week.

Married women and widows who do not qualify for a basic pension in their own right may be entitled to a basic pension on their husband's contributions at about 60 per cent of the level to which he is entitled (see 'Pensions for women' on page 94). Since the introduction of independent taxation, husband and wife are assessed separately for tax. As a result, a married woman is now entitled to have her section of the joint pension offset against her own personal allowance – instead of being counted as part of her husband's taxable income. For many pensioner couples, this should mean a reduction in their tax liability.

Reduced-rate contributions note. Many women retiring today may have paid a reduced-rate contribution under a scheme that was abolished in 1978. Women who were already paying a reduced-rate contribution were, however, allowed to continue doing so. These reduced-rate contributions do not count towards your pension and you will not have had any contributions credited to you. If you are still some years away from retirement, it could be to your advantage to cancel the reduced-rate option, as by doing so you may be able to build up a wider range of benefits without paying anything extra. This applies if you are currently (2008/09) earning between £90 and £105 a week, ie between the lower earnings limit and the primary threshold. If you are earning above the primary threshold (ie £105), to get the same extra benefits you would have to start paying extra contributions. For advice, contact your local tax office. Or see website: www.hmrc.gov.uk.

How your pension is worked out

Your total pension can come from three main sources: the basic pension, the additional pension and the graduated pension. Anyone wanting to work out what they are due can write to their pension centre for a 'pension forecast'. This is normally expressed in percentage terms, so, for instance, someone with full contributions will get 100 per cent of the pension. You can also get a forecast of the additional earnings-related pension to which you are entitled. To obtain a forecast, ring the Pension Service on Tel: 0845 3000 168 and request form BR19. Or, if more convenient, you can print off the form from the Pension Service website: www.thepension-service.gov.uk.

It is worth getting an early estimate of what your pension will be, as it may be possible to improve your NI contribution record by making additional Class 3 voluntary contributions. Although these can normally only be paid for six years in arrears, the time limit for missed contributions from April 1996 to 2001 has been extended but is likely to end in either 2009 or 2010, depending on when State Pension age was reached. However, since married people can use the spouse's contribution record to improve their pension, they will need to work out whether paying the extra would be worthwhile. Check with the Pension Service (see above).

The full basic pension for a man or woman (April 2008/09) is £90.70 a week, and it is £145.05 for a married couple (unless your spouse is entitled to more than the £54.35 spouse's addition on his/her own contributions, in which case you will receive more). Pensions are uprated in April each year. Up-to-date rates are contained in leaflet RM1 *Retirement – A guide to benefits for people who are retiring or have retired*, obtainable from your pension centre and main Post Offices or see website: www.dwp. gov.uk. All pensions are taxable other than one or two special categories, such as war widows and the victims of Nazism. If, however, your basic pension is your only source of income, you will not have to worry as the amount you receive is below the income tax threshold.

The rate of the basic pension depends on your record of NI contributions over your working life. To get the full rate you must have paid (or been credited with) NI contributions for roughly nine-tenths of your working life, although widows can also be entitled to a full basic pension on their husband's contributions. If you are divorced, you may be able to use your former spouse's contributions to improve your own pension entitlement, provided that you have not remarried before reaching pension age.

Your working life, for this purpose, is normally considered to be 39 years for a woman and 44 years for a man, but it may be less if you were of working age but not in insurable employment when the National Insurance Scheme started in 1948. In 2006 the government announced a cut in the number of years' NI contributions needed to qualify for the full basic pension to 30 from the year 2010. Those who reach pension age earlier than the date these rules come into force, however, will *not* benefit.

Reduced-rate pension

If you do not have full contributions but have maintained your contributions record for between a quarter and nine-tenths of your working life, you may get a pension at a reduced rate. The amount is calculated according to the number of years for which you have paid contributions. However, to get any basic pension you must satisfy two conditions. First, you must actually have paid enough full-rate contributions in any one tax year, from 6 April 1975, for that year to count as a qualifying year; or have paid 50 flat-rate contributions, in any one year, before 6 April 1975. Second, your total contributions must be enough to have entitled you to at least 25 per cent of the full basic rate.

Additional pension: SERPS

SERPS, the additional State Pension scheme, was discontinued by the government in April 2002 and has been replaced by a new additional scheme, called the State Second Pension. Those formerly contracted into SERPS will not suffer any loss, as they will still keep the benefit of any contributions made. Equally, of course, those already in receipt of a SERPS pension will continue to receive their payments as normal. If you paid into the scheme, you probably know that the amount of additional pension you will get depends on your earnings above an annually adjusted 'lower earnings limit' for each complete tax year since April 1978.

If you have not already done so, it would be sensible to apply for a statement of your savings in SERPS by completing Form BR19 *Pension Forecast Application Form*, obtainable from any pension centre. Full details and examples of how SERPS is worked out can be found in leaflet PM2 *State Pensions – Your guide*, obtainable by calling the Pensions Info-Line on Tel: 0845 731 3233 / 0845 60 60 265 or see the website of the Pension Service: www.thepension-service.gov.uk.

In practical terms, the fact that SERPS has been discontinued may make very little difference to your plans. You can remain in the additional State Pension scheme, ie the State Second Pension. Or, as before, if you think you can do better by making independent provision, you can invest instead in either a personal pension or stakeholder pension. For details, see 'Personal pension schemes' and 'Stakeholder pensions', pages 71 and 78.

SERPS benefits for surviving spouses. The rules about inheriting a SERPS pension changed in October 2002, so they may have changed since you last worked out what pensions you will get. The changes are being gradually phased in up to October 2010. Additionally, anyone who was over State pension age on 5 October 2002 will be exempt from any cuts and will keep the right to pass on their SERPS pension in full to a bereaved spouse however many years away the bereavement may be. Equally, any younger widow, or widower who had already inherited a late spouse's SERPS entitlement before 6 October 2002 will not be affected and will continue to receive the full amount. The Department for Work and Pensions (DWP) table below shows how the cuts apply to those reaching State pension age between October 2002 and 2010. For further information, see leaflet SERPSL1 *Important Information for Married People – Inheritance of SERPS*, available from your local pension centre – Tel: 0845 60 60 265; www.thepensionservice.gov.uk.

SERPS passing to surviving spouse (%)	Date when contributor reaches State pension age
100	5 October 2002 or earlier
90	6 October 2002 – 5 October 2004
80	6 October 2004 – 5 October 2006
70	6 October 2006 – 5 October 2008
60	6 October 2008 – 5 October 2010
50	6 October 2010 or later

State Second Pension (S2P)

The State Second Pension replaced SERPS from April 2002. If you were previously contributing to SERPS, you are unlikely to have noticed very much difference. Your future additional pension will continue to be worked out on earnings on which you have paid Class 1 contributions as an employee. Class 1 contributions are paid (or credited) as a percentage of earnings, currently (2008/09) between £90 and £770 a week.

In time this will change as, a few years from now, the pension payments are planned to become flat-rate instead of earnings-related. The State Second Pension gives employees earning up to a certain amount (£31,100 in 2008/09) a better pension than SERPS, whether or not they are contracted-out into a private pension, with most help going to those on the lowest earnings (up to around £13,500 in 2008/09).

The main beneficiaries of the S2P will be: 1) people earning up to around £13,500, who will be able to save towards a much better pension; and 2) some carers and people with a long-term illness or disability, who will receive credits, equivalent to their earning £13,500, for periods when owing to their caring responsibilities or ill-health they are unable to work. Others likely to gain are employees with earnings up to about £31,100 who should be able to look forward to a more generous additional pension than with SERPS.

The State Second Pension is not applicable to the self-employed, for whom the alternative pension choices are either a personal pension or a stakeholder pension. However, this may change, as the government has announced proposals to allow the self-employed to join S2P in return for higher National Insurance contributions.

If you are a member of a contracted-out occupational pension scheme, you are legally entitled either to a pension that must be broadly the same, or better, than you would have got under the State scheme, or to what are known as protected rights (ie your and your employer's compulsory contributions to your pension together with their accumulated investment growth).

Graduated pension

This pension existed between April 1961 and April 1975.

The amount you receive depends on the graduated NI contributions you paid during that period. Anyone over 18 and earning more than £9 a week at that time will probably be entitled to a small graduated pension. This includes married women and widows with reduced contribution liability. A widow or widower whose spouse dies when they are both over pension age can inherit half of the graduated pension based on their late spouse's contributions.

Ways to increase your pension

Deferring your pension. Your pension will be increased if you delay claiming it past State retirement age. You can do so whether you are still in work or not. For every year you defer taking your pension, there will be an increase in its value. For example, if you put off claiming your State pension for a year, when you do finally claim it you could get an extra 10.4 per cent added to your weekly State Pension for life – that's just over an extra £1 for every £10 of State Pension.

You can continue deferring your pension for as long as you like. The extra money will be paid to you when you eventually decide to claim your pension. You can choose whether to take it as a taxable lump sum or in higher weekly pension payments. If you choose to receive higher weekly payments, you will need to defer your pension for at least five weeks. If you go for the lump sum, deferral must be for at least one year; the rate of interest paid will be 2 per cent over bank rate. For further information, see leaflet SPD1 *Your Guide to State Pension Deferral: Putting off your state pension to get extra state pension or a lump sum payment later*, obtainable by ringing Tel: 0845 731 3233; or see the website: www.thepensionservice.gov.uk.

Warning. If you plan to defer your pension, you should also defer any graduated pension to which you may be entitled – or you risk losing the increases you would otherwise obtain.

Increases for dependants. Your basic pension may be increased if you are supporting a dependent spouse or children. Most typically, this applies in respect of a non-working wife (or one whose earnings are very low) who is under 60 when her husband retires. However, this also applies for a retired wife supporting a husband dependent by reason of invalidity. The current rates are £54.35 a week for a spouse, £8.75 for the first child and £11.35 each for any other dependent children. This is not available to new claims starting from 6 April 2003 or later. After that date no payments are made for any dependent children. The definition of a dependent child is one for whom you are receiving child benefit. If you think you might be entitled to an increase in respect of your spouse or children, complete form BF225 *Dependants Allowance*, obtainable from your pension centre.

Age addition. Your pension will be automatically increased once you reach 80. The current rate is 25p a week.

Income support

If you have an inadequate income, you may qualify for

income support. There are special premiums (ie additions) for lone parents, disabled people, carers and pensioners.

A condition of entitlement is that you should not have capital, including savings, of more than £16,000. To qualify for maximum income support, the capital limit is £6,000. For every £500 of capital over £6,000, individuals are deemed to be getting £1 a week income – so the actual amount of benefit will be reduced accordingly. A big advantage is that people entitled to income support receive full help with their rent and should also not have any council tax to pay.

NB. All pensioners are guaranteed at least a minimum income. This used to be known as Minimum Income Guarantee (MIG). It has been superceded by the Pension Credit and is officially called Pension Credit Guarantee Credit (see below). Single pensioners are guaranteed £124.05 a week, and couples £189.35. These totals exclude mortgage interest and disregarded income; for example, attendance allowance. If you were previously receiving Minimum Income Guarantee, you should now automatically be getting the guaranteed element of Pension Credit. If for some reason this is not happening or if though previously eligible you failed to claim it, ring the Pension Credit Helpline on Tel: 0800 991 234 or check their website: www.thepensionservice.gov.uk.

Pension Credit

The Pension Credit was introduced in October 2003. As explained above, it incorporates a guaranteed element (ie the previous Minimum Income Guarantee) plus an addition designed to reward pensioners with modest savings. It benefits single people aged 65-plus with a weekly income of up to £174 and couples with an income of up to £255 (2008/09) by increasing the standard guaranteed amount to include a bonus to make saving worthwhile. In cash terms, the credit is worth up to £19.71 a week for single people and up to £26.13 for couples. If you are not already receiving Pension Credit but think you would be entitled to do so, ring the Pension Credit Helpline on T: 0800 991 234 (8 am to 8 pm, Monday to Friday; 9 am to 1 pm, Saturday), or check their website: www.thepensionservice.gov.uk. If you prefer, you can get an application form from any pension centre. At the same time, you might like to ask for leaflet PC1L *Pension Credit – Pick it up it's yours*. To help ensure that no one entitled to the credit misses out, claims can be backdated 12 months.

Social Fund. If you are faced with an exceptional expense you find difficult to pay, you may be able to obtain a Budgeting or Crisis Loan, or Funeral Payment, from the Social Fund. Ask at your social security or Jobcentre Plus office. Website: www.jobcentreplus.gov.uk.

Working after you start getting your pension

This used to be a problem for many people as a result of the Earnings Rule. At the time, men between the ages of 65 and 69 and women between the ages of 60 and 64 who earned more than £75 a week had their basic State pension reduced. Happily, this does not apply any more and today there is no longer any limit to the amount pensioners can earn.

Early retirement and your pension

Because so many people retire early, there is a widespread belief that it is possible to get an early pension. Although the information is correct as regards many employers' occupational pension schemes, as well as for stakeholder and personal pensions, it does not apply to the basic State Pension. If you take early retirement before the age of 60, it may be necessary for you to pay voluntary Class 3 NI contributions in order to protect your contributions' record for pension purposes. If you are a man over 60, however, you will automatically get contribution credits from the tax year in which you reach 60.

How you get a pension

You should claim your pension a few months before you reach State pension age. The Department of Work and Pensions (DWP) should send you a claim form (BR1) at the proper time, but if this doesn't arrive, it is your responsibility to contact them. Remember they will send the claim form to the last recorded address they hold for you, so if you have moved and not informed them, do make sure they have your current address. You should apply for the form about four months before you are due to retire. Or, if you prefer, instead of using a claim form you can ring the Pensions Service claim line on Tel: 0845 300 1084 and give your details over the phone or get in touch with them online: www.pensionservice.gov.uk. After you claim, you are told in writing exactly how much pension you will get. You will also be told what to do if you disagree with the decision. The information you are given should include the name and address of the organisation responsible for paying you any guaranteed extra pension (ie the equivalent of what you would have received from the additional State Pension).

How your pension can be paid

Pensions are usually paid direct into a bank account, rather than by order books and giros. You can choose whether it is a bank or building society account or, if you prefer, a Post Office Card Account. Those who want to do so can still collect their pension from the Post Office, though if you have a bank or building society account you will need to check whether your account offers this facility. All recipients whose pension is not already being paid direct will be notified by letter when they need to decide on an account and how if necessary they can arrange to open one. In the meantime, if you have a pension book or use giros, you can continue collecting your pension as normal.

NB. Although most people who have already made the switch to direct payment find it safer and more convenient, there were fears that some more vulnerable pensioners would genuinely be unable to manage an account. The government has recognised this and individuals in this situation can still receive their money every week by cheque, which can be cashed at the Post Office or paid direct into a Post Office Card Account.

Other situations. If your pension is £5 a week or less, it will normally be paid once a year in arrears by a crossed order that you can pay into a bank or building society account. Payment is made each year shortly before Christmas. Pensions can be paid to an overseas address, if you are going abroad for six months or more. For further details see leaflets NI38 *Social Security Abroad*, obtainable from HMRC (NI Contributions) offices and GL29 *Going Abroad and Social Security Benefits*, obtainable from social security and pension centre offices; website: www.pensionservice. gov.uk. If you are in hospital, your pension can still be paid to you. Until recently, the amount was reduced if you were in hospital for more than 52 weeks, but since April 2006 this is no longer the case. You now can receive your pension in full for the duration of your stay, regardless of how long you have to remain in hospital. Leaflet GL12 *Going Into Hospital?* (obtainable from Jobcentre Plus offices and NHS hospitals) provides full information; website: www.job centreplus.gov.uk.

Christmas bonus

Pensioners usually get a small tax-free bonus shortly before Christmas each year. The amount and due date is announced in advance. For many years the sum has been £10. The bonus is combined with your normal pension payment for the first week in December.

Advice

If you have any queries or think you may not be obtaining your full pension entitlement, you should contact the Pensions Service as soon as possible. If you think a mistake has been made, you have the right to appeal and can insist on your claim being heard by an independent tribunal.

Before doing so, you would be strongly advised to consult a solicitor at the Citizens Advice Bureau or the Welfare Advice Unit of your social security office. Some areas have special Tribunal Representation Units to assist people to make claims at tribunals. If you are contacting the Pensions Service with a query, you should quote either your National Insurance number (or your spouse's) or your pension number if you have already started receiving your pension. For further information about pensions, see leaflets RM1 *Retirement – A guide to benefits for people who are retiring or have retired* and PM2 *State Pensions – Your guide*, obtainable by calling the Pensions Information Line on Tel: 0845 731 3233 or see the website: www.pensionservice. gov.uk.

Private pensions

The importance of persuading individuals to save for their own pension instead of just relying on the State has been recognised by successive governments. Encouragement has been made through tax incentives so that, despite recent problems, pension savings are still one of the most tax effective investments available:

▇ you get income tax relief on contributions at your highest tax rate;

▓ the pension fund is totally exempt from income tax and capital gains tax, providing good growth prospects for your money;

▓ part of the pension can be taken as a cash sum when you retire and that too is tax free.

Private pension schemes fall into two broad categories: those arranged by employers, for example company pension schemes, and those you can arrange for yourself.

Company pension schemes

About 10 million people are now participating in company pension schemes. Although these can vary considerably, the following basic features apply to all of them.

Pension fund. Pension contributions go into a pension fund that is quite separate from your employer's company. It is set up under trust and run by trustees, appointed from management and from pension scheme members. It is the job of the trustees to manage the fund and its investments and to ensure that the benefit promises are kept.

Payments into the fund. Your scheme may or may not ask for a contribution from you. For this reason, schemes are known as 'contributory' or 'non-contributory'. If (as is normally the case) you are required to make a contribution, this will be deducted from your pay before you receive it.

Your employer's contributions to the scheme represent the money your employer is setting aside for your pension and other benefits. In some schemes the amount is calculated as a fixed percentage of your earnings. In others the scheme actuary would estimate the amount that your employer needs to pay to ensure your (and other members') benefits in the future.

Benefits from the scheme. All pension scheme members should be given a booklet describing how the scheme works, what benefits it provides and other information, including the address of the Pensions Ombudsman. If you do not receive one, you should ask the person in the company responsible for the pension scheme – this is often the personnel manager – to supply you with a booklet. You can also ask to see a copy of the trust deed as well as the latest annual report and audited accounts. The key benefits applicable to most pension schemes include:

■ a pension due at whatever age is specified by the scheme, usually somewhere between 60 and 65 (although many companies offer early retirement provision);

■ Death benefit (sometimes known as lump sum life assurance), paid out if you die before retirement age;

■ A widow's/widower's pension paid for life no matter when you die. **NB:** Since December 2005, same-sex couples who enter a civil partnership by officially registering their relationship are treated the same as married couples, which among other benefits entitles them to receive an equivalent survivor's pension to that of a married person on the death of their partner.

Contribution and benefit limits. The government sets limits (for tax relief) on the contributions that individuals can invest in their pension plan and on the pension benefits they can receive. Prior to April 2006, the rules differed between one type of scheme and another. These anomalies have now been swept away, as the government has brought all company and personal pension schemes under a single tax regime.

Among other important changes, the earnings cap is no longer a factor. Instead, individuals can now invest up to 100 per cent of annual earnings into their plan (or plans) with the benefit of tax relief, up to a maximum figure – known as the annual allowance – of £235,000. Higher contributions are allowed but without any tax relief on the excess. There is also a lifetime limit of £1.65 million for total pension funds, including any fund growth. Funds in excess of the lifetime limit are subject to a 25 per cent recovery charge (ie tax) if taken as income, or 55 per cent if taken as a lump sum. Both the annual allowance and the lifetime limit will be increased in stages, rising respectively to £255,000 and £1.8 million by 2010/11.

Individuals whose pension fund was already over the lifetime limit before 6 April 2006 – or is anticipated to become so before they draw their pension – can protect their fund from the recovery charge, provided the fund is formally registered with HMRC within three years of 6 April 2006. Anyone wishing to apply for Primary or Enhanced Protection must do so **before 5 April 2009**.

Tax-free lump sum. Provided your scheme rules allow, you can take up to a maximum of 25 per cent of the value of your fund – including additional voluntary contributions (AVCs) and contracted-out benefits from the State Second Pension scheme – from age 50 (55 from 2010) without having to retire. Furthermore, unless you are in a final salary scheme, you are no longer obliged to take any pension income when accessing your lump sum but can leave the money in the fund to continue to grow. A major new benefit for those nearing retirement is that they can ease into part-time work, take their lump sum and, if they wish to do so, start drawing some pension income.

Scheme rules. The fact that HMRC has changed the rules is unfortunately no guarantee that individuals will be able to take full advantage of all the new options that have become available. Their employer's pension scheme rules will also need to have been altered accordingly, which may not always be the case. Before making any definite plans, it would be advisable to check with whoever is responsible for the company scheme.

Types of scheme

Most employers' schemes are of the final salary or money purchase type. Other types that exist are average earnings and flat-rate schemes.

Final salary scheme. Your pension is calculated as a propor-tion of your final pay, which could mean literally the last year you work, or possibly for controlling directors the average of three consecutive years during the last 10. The amount you receive depends on two factors: the number of years you have worked for the organisation plus the fraction

of final pay on which the scheme is based, typically ¹⁄₆₀th or
¹⁄₈₀th. So if you have worked 30 years for a company that has
¹⁄₆₀th pension scheme, you will receive ³⁰⁄₆₀ths of your final
pay – in other words, half. Final pay schemes can be
contracted into or out of the additional State Pension
scheme. If a scheme is contracted out, it must provide a
pension that is broadly equal to, or better than, its State
equivalent.

Money purchase scheme. Unlike final salary schemes, the
amount of pension you receive is not based on a fixed
formula but (within HMRC limits) is dependent on the
investment performance of the fund into which your own
and your employer's contributions on your behalf have been
paid.

Although there is an element of risk with money purchase
schemes, in that no one can forecast with certainty how well
or badly a pension fund might do, in practice most trustees
act very conservatively.

Different schemes have different ways of determining how
members' pension entitlements are calculated. You should
enquire what the rules are and additionally (if you have not
already received one) you should request a Statutory Money
Purchase Illustration (SMPI), which should give you an idea
of what size pension you might realistically expect once
inflation has been taken into account. You should receive a
fresh SMPI statement every year, based on the actuarial
assumptions that have been used to calculate its growth and
the (inflation-adjusted) income it should yield on purchase
of an annuity. One of the more important changes of the
new rules is that it is no longer compulsory to purchase an

annuity. Individuals who prefer to keep their fund invested can opt, at 75, for an alternatively secured pension.

Group personal pension scheme. Employers sometimes arrange group schemes for employees wishing to build up a personal pension. They are usually more advantageous than individual personal pensions because employers normally make contributions of 3 per cent (or more) into all participants' pension fund. Also, because of the group savings, the charges tend to be lower than for individually administered schemes. All personal pensions, whether group or individual, are a form of money purchase scheme.

Contracted-out mixed benefit scheme (COMBS). This is a mixed scheme that combines elements of salary-related and money purchase schemes.

Average earnings scheme. As its name implies, this is based on your average earnings over the total period of time that you are participating in the scheme. Every year, an amount goes into the scheme on your behalf, calculated in accordance with your level of earnings. As your salary increases, so too do your potential benefits. Each year, your 'profits' from the scheme are worked out from a formal table and the total of all these annual sums constitutes your pension.

Flat-rate pension scheme. Your level of pay is not a factor. Instead, the same flat rate applies to everyone, multiplied by the number of years in which they have been participants of the scheme. So, for example, if the flat rate is £500 a year of pension and you have been a member of the scheme for 20 years, your pension will be £10,000 a year.

Useful organisation. There is an organisation that is committed to helping anyone who has an occupational pension in the United Kingdom. It has over 100,000 members, who benefit from having a powerful voice representing their interests. Unite is the largest member of the Occupational Pensioners' Alliance and offers support to its members through campaigns, helplines, networks and representation. For further information contact: Tel: 01582 721652; e-mail: info@pensioneronline.com; website: www. pensioneronline.com.

Executive pension plans

These are individual pension plans arranged by an employer for the benefit of some or all executives above a certain grade. In some companies, executive pension plans only apply to directors; in others, they may also include senior and middle management. Equally, there may be a separate policy for each individual, or a master policy covering everyone in the scheme.

One of the attractions of executive pension plans is their potential flexibility. They can be tailored to cater for differing retirement ages as well as for varying contribution levels, which explains why some organisations are able to offer early retirement on very attractive terms.

Historically, executive pension plans are of the money purchase type and the same government-allowable contribution and benefit rules equally apply to them as to other pension schemes. Normally, one of the following four types of investment policy is used: with profits, unit linked, deposit administration and non-profit.

Possible changes to your scheme

Unfortunately, many employers have recently been closing their final salary schemes to new entrants and even, in some cases, discontinuing them for existing members – replacing them instead with money purchase schemes. Although there is no pretending that money purchase schemes are as good as final salary ones, you will almost certainly be better off remaining in your employer's scheme than leaving it in favour of, say, a personal pension. Your employer will still be making contributions into the scheme on your behalf, which very few employers do in the case of personal pensions, and additionally you will not have any manage-ment charges to pay, which if you had a personal pension, would come out of your own fund. Also, if you fear that your pension will be insufficient, you have several possible ways of helping to improve it: you can make AVCs; you can invest in a stakeholder scheme (this is now allowed even if you have earnings of more than £30,000); or you can invest in a personal pension. If you like, you can do all three.

Focus on high earners

Most of the previous rules affecting high earners, in partic-ular the earnings cap and the allowable tax-free lump sum, have been swept away. In common with everyone else, their maximum tax-free lump sum is now limited to 25 per cent of their fund value or 25 per cent of their lifetime limit, whichever is lower. For many high earners, this is likely to be a positive gain. But not all pension schemes have changed their rules accordingly, so, when it comes to the lump sum, this might well be a point to check. Equally, a couple of other former rules may well still apply. In particular, until recently, high earners who joined a new pension scheme were required to base their final salary assessment on their average earnings over any three consecutive years during their last 10. Similarly, controlling directors were not permitted to resign just before retirement to boost their salary but, instead, had to use the three-year average method of calculation. Also, gains from share options in the final year of employment were not allowed in the calculation of final salary.

Accelerated accrual rates. Some schemes allow individuals to enjoy an enhanced accrual scale to qualify for full pension benefits after an agreed minimum number of years service.

Top-up schemes. Employers can still set up 'top-up' pension schemes to provide additional benefits above the HMRC limits, but such schemes are now taxable and their former advantages have largely gone as a result of the new pension rules introduced in 2006. There is some transitional relief for individuals with existing schemes. If you have a FURBS (funded, unapproved retirement benefit scheme), SUURBS (secured, unfunded, unapproved retirement benefit scheme) or similar, expert advice is strongly recommended to explore your best course of action.

Pension pot of less than £15,000

People with a pension pot of under £15,000 once they reach 60 can take all the money as a lump sum – with a quarter of their lump sum being tax-free and the remainder subject to income tax. If annuity rates are still at their current low, some individuals might be better off paying the tax. Your pension provider, or an independent financial adviser (IFA), should be able to advise you at the time. An important point if you have more than one pension plan is that the 'exempt' amount of £15,000 does not apply to each of them but is the total aggregate value of all your plans. If you wish to take a lump sum from all of them, this will need to have been arranged within a 12-month period, at any time between age 60 and 75.

Additional voluntary contributions (AVCs)

If, as you approach retirement, you become aware that you are not going to have a big enough pension to live as comfortably as you would like, you might seriously consider the possibility of making AVCs. Although no longer as valuable as they once were, because the 2006 rule-changes allow individuals similar ways of boosting their pension, nevertheless for some people AVCs might still offer the best solution. Their particular attractions are, first, that AVCs – as well as the growth of the plan – enjoy full tax relief, so for basic-rate taxpayers HMRC is in effect paying £22 of every £100 invested. A further advantage is that some AVCs allow you to purchase 'added years', to make up any shortfall in your entitlement to benefit under a company scheme.

However, as you are probably aware, an option known as 'free-standing AVCs' is also on offer. As the name implies, these are not linked to a company scheme but can be purchased independently from insurance companies, building societies, banks, unit trusts, friendly societies and independent financial advisers. Individuals can, if they wish, contribute both to company AVCs and to a free-standing plan or plans (FSAVCs). To enjoy the tax relief, the total of all your AVCs plus other contributions to the pension plan is not allowed to exceed your annual earnings; or your annual allowance, if this is lower.

Rule changes. Over the years, there have been several rule changes of which you should be aware:

■ Previously, individuals had to make a commitment to pay regular contributions for a period of at least five years. This requirement has been abolished and (provided the actual scheme rules permit) both the amount and timing of payments can be varied to suit members according to their personal circumstances.

■ AVCs purchased between April 1987 and 5 April 2006 could not be used towards the tax-free lump sum but had to be taken as part of an individual's regular pension income. This rule has been abolished and AVC plans can now go towards your pension or towards your lump sum, as you prefer.

■ Until a few years ago, AVC benefits could only be taken at the same time as the other main benefits from an occupational pension scheme. Today, provided your scheme rules allow, the benefit can be taken at any time between ages 50 and 75 (or earlier if an individual is forced to leave employment due to incapacity). If you choose to draw your AVC benefits before you retire, they would normally have to be taken as part of your tax-free lump sum or in the form of income drawdown (see page 52–53).

Choosing an AVC plan. A number of recent reports have suggested that the claims made for AVCs often fall well short of the mark. The main criticisms are variously: 1) the poor performance of some AVC schemes; and 2) the high charges that in extreme cases have left investors with a negative return. By contrast, the best schemes can yield excellent value and for many individuals can be one of the most effective ways of increasing their security in retirement. Anyone advising you about the purchase of FSAVCs must at very least explain the basic differences between the FSAVCs being recommended and the AVCs offered by your employer's scheme.

Independent financial advisors (IFAs) must go further and give you an analysis of the specific differences to help you decide which type of scheme – or possible alternative type of investment – would be in your best financial interest. As with any other important investment decision, you would be well advised to take your time, do some basic research into the track record of any policies you might be considering (specialist publications such as *Money Management* provide a good starting point) and on no account sign any document without first being absolutely certain that you fully understand all the terms and conditions. Finally, if you are already subscribing to company AVCs, before investing in a new plan check on your present level of contributions and the benefits that these are expected to yield. You should be aware that current taxation, legislation and HMRC practice are all liable to change without notice and the impact of taxation (and any tax reliefs) depends on individual circumstances. Please check details with your company pension adviser or IFA, who should be only too happy to answer any questions.

Early leavers

In the past early leavers tended to do very badly, due to the heavy financial penalties of withdrawing from a scheme in mid-term. In recent years, however, the government has introduced new rules that help considerably. For example, employers can now pay full pension, without actuarial reduction, at any age between 50 and 70. Companies are under no obligation to do so but, for those people lucky enough to work for an organisation that has amended its pension scheme rules accordingly, this provision could make an immense difference to the financial position of early retirees.

Another important change concerns what are known as your preserved rights – in other words, your financial rights with regard to your pension. Today, the qualifying period is two years. If you leave earlier but have at least three months' qualifying service in the scheme, you now have a choice. Whereas previously the best you might have hoped for was a refund of contributions, today, if you prefer, you can request to have a cash sum transferred to another scheme. There are three choices available to people with preserved rights who leave a company to switch jobs.

Leaving the pension with the scheme. You remain a member of the scheme and receive a pension at the scheme's normal retirement age. If the scheme is a final salary one, the value would probably be calculated on 1/60th (or 1/80th) of your earnings at the time of your leaving and the number of years you have worked for the company. Whereas previously most pensions got frozen, today company schemes are obliged to increase the accrued pension rights by 2.5 per cent (5 per cent until 2005) a year or the rate of inflation, whichever is lower. Another advantage of remaining in the scheme is that you keep any benefits – such as a widow's pension and possibly others – that are already included. Also, once you start receiving your pension, you would be entitled to any extra increases that may be given. In the case of money purchase schemes, your accumulated assets would normally remain invested in the fund, hopefully growing every year to buy you a bigger pension on retirement. You would also be entitled to any benefit that the scheme provided under the rules.

Taking your pension to a new scheme. You do not have to make an immediate decision. You can transfer your pension scheme at any time, provided you do so more than a year before you retire. If you wish to switch to a new scheme, this could be to another company scheme, a personal pension or a stakeholder pension. Personal and stakeholder pensions are described on pages 71 and 78 respectively, so if you are interested in taking advantage of either of these you should read the section carefully. Here, we explain the various possibilities if you wish to join a scheme run by your new employer.

Early leavers now have the right to move their pension – or more precisely, its transfer value – to a new employer's scheme willing to accept it. The transfer value is the cash value of your current pension rights. Calculating this, however, can be problematic and early leavers are often at a disadvantage compared with those who remain in the scheme. Joining a new employer's scheme does not necessarily oblige you to transfer your previous benefits. In some circumstances, there may be very good arguments for leaving your existing benefits with your former scheme and joining your new employer's scheme from scratch for the remaining years that you are working. Since you could be at risk of giving up more than you stand to gain by transferring your benefits to a new scheme, expert advice is strongly recommended.

Taking your pension to an insurance company. If neither of the two previous options appeals, or your new company will not accept your old pension value into its own scheme, you can go independent and have the transfer value of your pension invested by a life company into a personal scheme. After deducting its charges, the life company would invest the balance of the money in the fund, or funds, of your choice.

Advice. Deciding on your best option is not easy, so before taking action you should at least consult your company pension scheme manager to give you an assessment of the likely value of your pension if you leave it in the scheme. An important point to bear in mind is that your present company scheme may include valuable extras, such as a spouse's pension, life cover and attractive early retirement terms in the event of ill-health.

If you are planning to switch, you will need to decide between a Section 32 buy-out, a personal pension or a stakeholder pension. Because this is a complex area – and making the wrong decision could prove expensive – independent expert advice is very strongly recommended. Particularly if a large sum of money is involved, it could pay you to get the advice of a pension consultant. For a list of those operating in your area, contact the Society of Pension Consultants; Tel:

020 7353 1688; email: john.mortimer@spc.uk.com; website:www.spc.uk.com.

Useful reading

Transferring a Pension to Another Scheme and Ill-health Early Retirement, obtainable from The Pensions Advisory Service: Tel: 0845 601 2923; website: www.pensionsadvisoryservice.org.uk.

Leaflet PM4 *Personal Pensions – Your guide*, obtainable by calling the Pensions Info-Line on Tel: 0845 731 3233; website: www.thepensionservice.gov.uk.

Stakeholder Pensions and Decision Trees, obtainable from the Financial Services Authority, Tel: 0845 606 1234; website: www.fsa.gov.uk.

Minimum retirement age

At the present time, many company pension schemes allow you to take early retirement and draw your pension from the age of 50. But the minimum age is rising by five years to 55 with effect from 2010.

Questions on your pension scheme

Most people find it very difficult to understand how their pension scheme works. However, your pension may be worth a lot of money and, especially as you approach retirement, it is important that you should know the main essentials, including any options that may still be available to you.

If you have a query (however daft it may seem) or if you are concerned in some way about your pension, you should approach whoever is responsible for the scheme in your organisation. If the company is large, there may be a special person to look after the scheme on a day-to-day basis: this could be the pensions manager or, quite often, it is someone in the personnel department. In a smaller company, the pension scheme may be looked after by the company secretary or managing director. The sort of questions you might ask will vary according to circumstances, such as: before you join the scheme; if you are thinking of changing jobs; if you are hoping to retire early and so on.

If you stay until normal retirement age

▓ What will your pension be on your present salary? And what would it be assuming your salary increases by, say, 5 or 10 per cent before you eventually retire?

▓ What spouse's pension will be paid? Can a pension be paid to other dependants?

▓ Similarly, can a pension be paid to a partner – male or female?

▓ What happens if you continue working with the organisation after retirement age? Normally, any contributions you are making to the scheme will cease to be required and your pension (which will not usually be paid until you retire) will be increased to compensate for its deferment. **NB**: Since April 2006, provided their scheme rules allow it, members of occupational pension schemes can draw their pension benefits, if they wish, without having to wait until after they leave.

▓ What are the arrangements if you retire from the organisation as a salaried employee but become a retained consultant or contractor?

If you just want information

▓ Are any changes envisaged to the scheme? For example, if it is a final salary type, is there any chance that it might be wound up and a money purchase one offered instead?

▓ If there were a new money purchase scheme, would the company be making the same contributions as before or would these be lower in future?

▓ Is there any risk that benefits – either members' own or those for dependants – could be reduced?

▓ Is there a possibility that members might be required to pay higher contributions than at present?

What to do before retirement

In addition to understanding your current pension scheme, you may also need to chase up any previous schemes of which you were a member. This is well worth pursuing as you could be owed money from one or more schemes, which will all add to your pension on retirement day. You may be able to get the information from your previous employer(s). If you have difficulty in locating them – perhaps because the company has been taken over – contact the Pension Tracing Service, which assists individuals who need help in tracing their pension rights. This is a free service, run by the Pension Service, part of the Department for Work and Pensions. Its database contains the details of over 200,000 occupational and personal pension scheme administrators.

Applicants should contact the Pension Tracing Service, Tel: 0845 600 2537 or via the website: www.thepensionservice.gov.uk. If you have difficulty with your hearing or speech, you can call the Pension Tracing Service on Tel: 0845 3000 169. It is also possible to fill out a tracing request form online by visiting the website: www.thepension service.gov.uk and choose the link to the Pension Tracing Service.

Other help and advice

If you have any queries or problems to do with your pension, in addition to the Pension Tracing Service there are three main sources of help available to you. These are: the trustees or managers of your pension scheme, The Pensions Advisory Service and the Pensions Ombudsman.

Trustees or managers. These are the first people to contact if you do not properly understand your benefit entitlements or if you are unhappy about some point to do with your pension. Pensions managers (or other persons responsible for pensions) should give you their names and tell you how they can be reached.

The Pensions Advisory Service. This is an independent voluntary organisation with a network of 500 professional advisers throughout the United Kingdom. It can give free help and advice, other than financial advice, on all matters to do with any type of pension scheme. The service is available to any member of the public who either has a specific query or just needs general information. It operates a local call rate helpline: Tel: 0845 601 2923; or you can visit the website: www.thepensionsadvisoryservice.org.uk.

Pensions Ombudsman. You would normally approach the Ombudsman only if neither the pension scheme manager (or trustees) nor The Pensions Advisory Service are able to solve your problem. The Ombudsman can investigate: 1) complaints of maladministration by the trustees, managers or administrators of a pension scheme or by an employer; 2) disputes of fact or law with the trustees, managers or an employer. He does not, however, investigate: complaints about mis-selling of pension schemes, a complaint that is already subject to court proceedings, one that is about a State social security benefit or a dispute that is more appropriate for investigation by another regulatory body. There is also a time limit for lodging complaints, which is normally within three years of the act, or failure to act, about which you are complaining.

Provided the problem comes within the Ombudsman's orbit, he will look into all the facts for you and will inform you of his decision, together with his reasons. There is no charge for the Ombudsman's service. The Pensions Ombudsman has now also taken on the role of Pension Protection Fund Ombudsman and will be dealing with complaints about, and appeals from, the Pension Protection Fund. He will also be dealing with appeals from the Financial Assistance Scheme. Contact **The Pensions Ombudsman:** Tel: 020 7834 9144; website: www.pensions-ombudsman.org.uk. If you have a **personal pension,** contact the **Financial Ombudsman Service (FOS):** Tel: 0845 080 1800. It is possible you may be referred to the Pensions Ombudsman above, but if so you will be informed very quickly.

Protection for pension scheme members

New rules have been introduced to protect pension scheme members in the event of a company takeover or proposed bulk transfer arrangement. A welcome reform is that, in the event of a scheme in deficit being wound up, the deficiency becomes a debt on the employer that the trustees can pursue. As an additional safeguard, self-investment by occupational pension funds is now restricted to 5 per cent. Equally important, solvent companies choosing to wind up their scheme on or since 11 June 2003 will need to protect members' accrued pension rights in full.

The regulatory system has also become much more stringent since April 2005, with the creation of the **Pensions Regulator,** a body with wide powers and a proactive approach to regulation, whose top priority is to identify and tackle risks to members' benefits. There is now also a **Pension Protection Fund (PPF)** to help final salary pension scheme members who are at risk of losing their pension benefits due to their employer's insolvency. Members over the normal pension age will receive 100 per cent of their current benefits plus annual increases (the lower of RPI or 2.5 per cent) on pensions accrued from 6 April 1997.

Members below the scheme's normal retirement age will receive 90 per cent of the Pension Protection Fund level of compensation plus annual increases, subject to a cap and the standard Fund rules. There is more help too for members who lost pension savings in a company scheme before the introduction of the Pension Protection Fund. The **Financial Assistance Scheme (FAS)** offers help to some people who have lost out on their pension. The scheme is managed by the Department for Work and Pensions and is administered by the FAS Operational Unit (FAS OU). It makes payments to top up scheme benefits to eligible members of schemes that are winding up or have wound up. Assistance is also payable to the survivor of a pension scheme member. On 4 June 2008 as a result of the Financial Assistance Scheme (Miscellaneous Provisions) Regulations 2008, eligible members' scheme benefits were topped up to 90 per cent of their accrued pension (subject to a cap of £26,000 per annum). This is payable from normal retirement age (subject to a lower age limit of 60 and an upper age limit of 65).

Personal pensions for employees

A main aim behind personal pensions is to give people working for an employer the same freedom as the self-employed to make their own independent pension arrangements, should they wish to do so. Before making any decision, a basic point to understand is that nearly everyone who pays NI contributions as an employee is already contributing towards an additional pension: either to the State Second Pension or to a contracted-out company pension scheme.

You have the right to take a personal pension (PP) in place of the State Second Pension, or alternatively in place of your employer's scheme (whether this is contracted-in or -out). If you like you can also invest in a personal pension in addition to your employer's scheme, provided the total of your contributions does not exceed your annual allowance.

To judge whether a personal pension is a good idea, you need to understand the advantages and possible limitations of your present arrangements compared with the attractions – but also risks – of a PP. **If you are a member of a good contracted-out final salary scheme – or have the opportunity of joining one – it is very unlikely that a PP would be in your best interest.** If, however, your employer does not have a pension scheme, if you are ineligible to join, if the scheme is contracted into the State scheme, if you think you could do better for yourself than your current scheme or that it could be to your advantage to have an extra pension, then a PP might be worth considering.

A main advantage of a personal pension is that if you change jobs you can take it with you without penalty. You will have real choice as to how your pension payments are invested. If you have built up a big enough fund, you can retire at any age between 50 (55 from 2010) and 75. Also, if you change your mind after having taken a personal pension, you can switch back into the State scheme; or, if the scheme rules allow it, you can transfer your payments into a company contracted-out scheme.

The biggest drawback of a personal pension, particularly for an older person, is that it may not offer you such attractive benefits as your present scheme. For a start, most employers do not make extra contributions to a personal pension, so other than your rebate from the State Second Pension (see 'Minimum contributions' below), all the investment towards your pension will need to come out of your earnings. You may also lose out on valuable extra benefits that are often included in an employer's scheme, including: a pension before normal retirement age were you to become ill, protection for your dependants should you die, attractive early retirement terms if you were made redundant, any increases in pension payments that the scheme may give to help offset inflation.

Before taking a decision, a first essential is to understand how personal pensions work.

Starting date. You can decide to start a personal pension at any time you want and then, in order to receive all the minimum contributions that will be paid into your pension plan, backdate it to the start of the tax year on 6 April. The formalities involved are very easy.

Contributions into your pension plan. There are three possible ways (previously four, see 'special incentive payments' below) of building up savings in your pension plan:

■ **Minimum contributions.** These will be paid into your new scheme automatically. They are worked out according to the level of National Insurance contributions that both you and your employer are required to pay by law. Instead of going into either the State Second Pension or a contracted-out company pension scheme, they will be paid directly into your personal pension plan at the end of the income tax year to which they relate.

The older you are, the bigger the contribution rebate. Whereas previously there was a fixed percentage for all personal pension members (with those over 30 receiving an extra 1 per cent), since April 1997 contribution rebates are calculated on an age/earnings-related basis.

- **Extra contributions made by you.** You can make extra contributions into your pension plan. If you do so, you will not only build up more savings for your retirement but you also enjoy full tax relief on these contributions.

- **Voluntary contributions by your employer.** Your employer might decide that he/she wishes to help you improve your pension by making contributions over and above the statutory NI contributions into your pension plan. If you are considering leaving a company pension scheme, this could be one of the questions you should ask as a means of comparing the value of a personal pension against your existing scheme. The total of your and your employer's contributions is not allowed to exceed your annual earnings.

- **Special incentive payments.** An extra 2 per cent payment was given by the government as part of the launch of personal pensions. These payments have now ceased. Anyone who previously received them can look forward to enjoying the benefit when they retire.

Your pension receipts. As with all money purchase schemes, the amount of pension you eventually receive will depend on two main factors: the size of the fund you have been able to build up and the fund's investment performance. Generally speaking, the longer you have been saving towards a personal pension and the bigger the total contributions paid, the larger your pension will stand to be. Many pension advisers suggest that a useful formula is to halve your age at the time of first starting to save for your pension and use this figure as a percentage of your gross salary that you should invest annually in your pension for the remainder of your working life.

Thanks to the new A rules, you can average this out over the years, making lower contributions when money is tight and higher ones when you can more easily afford to do so. You have a great deal of choice in the matter but there are also certain rules designed to protect you.

A basic rule concerns what are known as your **protected rights**. These are the minimum contributions (including the value of the extra 2 per cent introductory payment) and tax relief you may have received – together with their accumulated investment growth. Your protected rights can only be invested in a single contract, in contrast to your/your employer's extra or voluntary contributions, which can be invested in as many different personal plans as you please. Since April 2006, you can choose whether to use your protected rights towards your annuity or towards your tax-free lump sum, as you prefer.

Choosing a pension plan. Personal pensions are offered by insurance companies, building societies, unit trusts, friendly societies and IFAs. Before you make up your mind, you should aim to look at a variety of plans. Furthermore, you should not hesitate to ask as many questions as you want about any points that are unclear or any technical term that you do not fully understand – including in particular any questions you may have about the level of charges.

Understanding the figures has become very much easier over the past few years. Today, not only are all life and pension policy providers required to state their charges in writing but they must also disclose any salesperson's commission – in cash terms – in advance of any contract being signed. These together with other essential 'consumer' information about the policy should be included in what are called the 'keyfacts' documents. Advisers must now also state in writing their reasons for any recommendations to you.

Because choosing both the right type of investment and the particular institution with which you are likely to feel happiest is such an important decision, even after you have chosen a scheme you will have a **14-day cooling off period** that gives you a chance to change your mind.

Is a personal pension a wise decision? This is a question that only you, or an adviser who knows your personal circumstances, can answer. As a general rule, if you are in a good company pension scheme the advice is to stay there. Those for whom opting out is likely to be least advised are older people in a good company or public sector pension scheme. The key issue is how your existing pension arrangements compare with the alternatives. For information about the value of your State scheme rights, complete form BR19 *State Pension Forecast* obtainable from your pension centre. Or check the Pension Service website at: www.thepension service.gov.uk.

In the case of an employer's scheme, ask the pensions department or the person responsible for pensions (this could be the personnel manager or company secretary) to provide you with full information about your pension and future benefits, including details of death and disability cover.

Other points you will need to consider include: what type of investment policy would suit you; what size contributions (within HMRC-allowed limits) you could realistically afford; and what, after deduction of administrative and other charges, your plan might be worth when you come to retire. This is not to say that taking a personal pension is either a right or a wrong decision, simply that you need to be aware of all the various factors before opting out of your present arrangements. Since the sums are often very complex, if you are thinking of making a change you would be strongly advised to consult an independent pensions specialist.

Useful reading

Leaflets QG1 *A Quick Guide to Pensions*, PM3 *Occupational Pensions – Your guide*, PM4 *Personal Pensions – Your guide* and PM5 *Pensions for the Self-Employed – Your guide*, obtainable by ringing Pensions Info-Line on Tel: 0845 731 3233; website: www.thepension-service.gov.uk.

Stakeholder Pensions and Decision Trees and *FSA Guide to Pensions*, obtainable free from the FSA, Tel: 0845 606 1234; website: www.fsa.gov.uk.

Stakeholder pensions

Stakeholder pensions were launched in April 2001 with the aim of encouraging more people to begin saving towards a pension. Stakeholders are very similar to personal pensions but with the advantage that they are required to meet specified government standards, including limiting maximum annual charges (excluding financial advice) to 1.5 per cent for the first 10 years of the policy. This was increased from 1 per cent in April 2005 but if you were investing in a stakeholder prior to this date, the maximum charge you would have to pay for the next few years will be held at 1 per cent.

Whereas until fairly recently pension contributions were always linked to earnings, anyone with a stakeholder policy can invest up to £3,600 a year, regardless of how much or how little they earn – or even if they have no earnings at all. A husband or wife could make contributions for a non-earning partner. Those wishing to contribute more than £3,600 a year to their own scheme can do so, provided they have earnings of over £3,600 a year. Also, savers can stop, start or alter payments without penalty.

All contributions paid will be net of basic-rate tax, with the pension provider reclaiming the tax from HM Revenue & Customs. Higher-rate taxpayers will need to reclaim the excess tax through the self-assessment system. **NB.** Because of the tax relief, the actual cost of a contribution worth £3,600 is £2,808. For higher-rate taxpayers, the cost is £2,160. From April 2008, when basic-rate tax reduced to 20 per cent, the cost for basic-rate taxpayers increased to £3,000. Most higher-rate taxpayers should be unaffected. However, as now, they will only be able to claim the excess relief if the stakeholder scheme is in their own name, rather than that of a partner or other person.

Early retirees who are already drawing an occupational pension can, if they wish, start contributing to a stakeholder pension. A good reason for doing so might be to take advantage of an immediate, or series of immediate, self-vesting pensions. As with personal pensions, stakeholder pensions can be taken at any age between 50 (55 from 2010) and 75.

How to obtain. Stakeholder pensions are available from banks, Post Offices, insurance companies and other financial institutions. Although the basic charges may not be very different between one provider and another, you are nevertheless strongly advised to investigate at least two or three plans and ask for much the same sort of information as you would if you were considering a personal pension. This is even more important if you are actually thinking of switching from a PP to a stakeholder pension or, as is possible, having a stakeholder as well as a PP.

Since weighing up the pros and cons of making a change is not easy, you are strongly recommended to get expert advice. Or if you have a particular query, contact the Pensions Advisory Service Helpline on Tel: 0845 601 2923; website: www.pensionsadvisoryservice.org.uk. Remember this organisation cannot give financial advice.

Useful reading

PM8 *Stakeholder Pensions – Your Guide*, obtainable from Pensions Info-Line on T: 0845 731 3233; website: www.the pensionservice.gov.uk.

Types of investment policy

There are four different types of investment policy: with-profits, unit-linked, deposit administration and non-profit policies. Brief descriptions of each follow.

With-profits policies. These are one of the safest types of pension investments. They guarantee you a known minimum cash fund and/or pension on your retirement and, although the guaranteed amount is not usually very high, bonuses are added at regular intervals, according to how the investments in the fund perform. Additionally, a terminal (or final) bonus is given when the pension policy matures. Over the past few years most terminal bonuses have been lower than projected, reflecting lowish interest rates and a patchy performance by equities. However, an important feature is that once bonuses are given, they cannot later be withdrawn or put at risk due to some speculative investment.

Unit-linked policies. These are less safe than with-profits policies but they offer the attraction of potentially higher investment returns. Unit-linked policies by and large have performed fairly well over the last 15 years and have conse-quently been growing in popularity. However, as illustrated by the recent stock market volatility, there is always the risk that they might not continue to perform as well in the future, and if there were a downturn, the size of your pension could obviously be affected. For this reason, many advisers recommend that their clients swap their unit-linked policies to the with-profits type about five years before they retire, provided market conditions are favourable at the time. The decision as to what is best will very much depend on timing. Clearly if the stock market is depressed, then cashing in equity-based contracts before you need could lose you money, unless of course your adviser takes the view that the stock market is likely to plunge even further. Another factor that will need to be taken into account is the prevailing level of interest rates, since these affect annuity rates.

Deposit administration policies. These lie somewhere between with-profits and unit-linked policies in terms of their risk/reward ratio. They operate rather like bank deposit accounts, where the interest rate is credited at regular intervals.

Non-profit policies. These have lost favour in recent years. Although they provide a guaranteed pension payment, the return on investment is usually very low. As a rule, they tend only to be recommended for people starting a plan within five years of their retirement.

Choosing the right policy. This is one area where it really pays to shop around. Great care is needed when choosing the organisation with which to invest your pension savings. Once you have committed yourself to a policy, you will not usually be able to move your money without considerable financial penalty. As a general rule, it is sensible to select a large, well-known company that has been in the market for a long time. Before deciding, you should compare several companies' investment track records. What you should look for is evidence of good, consistent results over a period of 10 to 20 years.

You should aim at the very least to talk to two or three financial institutions or independent financial advisers (IFAs) and make it clear to all of them that you are doing so. If you need further advice – and particularly if a large sum of money is involved – there could be a strong argument for consulting an independent pension consultant or IFA who charges fees rather than earns commission.

Another possibility is to set up your own **Self-Invested Personal Pension (SIPP)**. As the name implies, these are do-it-yourself schemes that among other assets can include directly held shares and commercial property. Contrary to the Chancellor's original announcement, residential property cannot be held in a SIPP (with the benefit of tax relief), nor can luxury items such as antiques, wine, classic cars and yachts. The big advantage of SIPPs is that they offer greater flexibility than ordinary pensions, but, against this, the administrative costs are usually far higher. Also, pension experts advise that such schemes are only suitable for fairly sophisticated investors with at least £100,000 in their pension fund. This is not to say that you should necessarily rule out SIPPS, simply that, before you go ahead, you should ensure that you understand the drawbacks as well as the advantages.

Complaints. If you have a complaint about advice you have received in relation to your SIPP or other personal pension, contact the Financial Ombudsman Service (FOS).

Opting back into the State scheme

You might have been told by a financial adviser that rather than continue with your personal pension, you may be better-off switching into the State Second Pension (S2P). One reason you might have been given is that the rebates paid to those who have contracted out of the State scheme are insufficient in the light of increased longevity and the expected return on equity investments. Another reason, quite simply, could be that your present fund is unlikely to yield you as good a pension as S2P, especially as the age-related rebates paid to those with personal pensions (and other money purchase schemes) have been reduced from 10.5 per cent to 7.4 per cent since April 2007.

The advice is most likely to be pertinent if you are already over 43 and have average, or modest, earnings. However, if you can afford to do so, there is nothing to stop you from contracting back into the State scheme and also having a personal pension. Before you decide, check that your adviser has taken account of all the factors. Particular points you might want to discuss include:

■ the likely value of your pension if you:

- stay as you are;

- contract back into the State scheme;

- contribute to both S2P and a personal pension.

■ what contributions you would need (or be advised) to make in each of the above situations;

▨ whether there would be a penalty if you stopped paying into your personal pension;

▨ how easy it would be to restart the plan should a PP be more advantageous when the State Second Pension changes from being earnings-related to flat-rate, as the government has planned to happen in the next few years.

Another point to take into account could be your financial adviser's charges, as these may come out of the fund that you are building towards your pension. As guidance, many PP managers have recently reduced their fees to around 1.5 per cent – in line with the norm (excluding financial advice) for stakeholder pensions.

A lump sum?

All pension scheme members, whether in an employer's scheme or having a private pension plan, are entitled to take a tax-free lump sum from their fund. The maximum amount allowed is 25 per cent of their fund or 25 per cent of their lifetime limit, whichever is lower. Although those with personal pensions have always been able to take their lump sum at any age between 50 and 75, members of employers' schemes normally had to wait until they retired. This is no longer so. Since April 2006, everyone (provided their scheme rules permit) can take their lump sum from age 50 without having to retire. Members of final salary schemes cannot, however, take their lump sum in isolation. A further point, of which you should be aware, is that the minimum age at which you can retire or take your lump sum is being raised from 50 to 55 next year, 2010.

Taking a lump sum reduces the pension you receive, but on the other hand, if you invest the money wisely, you could end up with a higher income. If you take a lump sum, the amount by which your pension will be reduced is mainly determined by your age. The younger you are, the smaller the reduction. Another consideration is your tax status. Since the lump sum is tax free, as a general rule the higher your top rate of tax after retirement, the greater the advantage in opting for a lump sum. Your life expectancy can also be an important factor. The shorter this is, the more sense it makes to take the lump sum, rather than deny yourself for a longer-term pension that you will not be around to enjoy.

Before consulting an expert, it would be helpful to both of you if you could work out – at least in very general terms – what your financial priorities are. The types of question your adviser will ask are: whether you are investing for income now or capital growth in the future; and what other sources of income you have, or might expect to receive. As is normal conservative practice, you will probably find that you will be recommended to spread your lump sum across a mixture of investments.

Pension rights if you continue to work after retirement age

When you reach normal retirement age, you will usually stop making contributions into your company pension scheme, even if you decide to carry on working. Your employer, of course, would have to agree to your continuing to work but, thanks to the age discrimination legislation, this should not normally be a problem if you are under 65 and are physically and mentally capable of doing your job. Even if you are over 65, you may find that your employer will be only too happy for you to stay – and, even then, if he/she wants you to leave, he/she will have to give you at least six months' notice in writing. If you are facing such a decision, here are some points to bear in mind:

■ You can continue working, draw your company pension and put some (or possibly all) of your earnings into a separate scheme.

■ You can leave your pension in the fund, where it will continue to earn interest until you retire. In most private schemes, you could expect to receive in the region of an extra 8 per cent for every year that you delay retirement. If you continue working, say for an additional five years, your pension would then be 40 per cent higher than if you had started taking it at the normal age. You will also have been earning a salary meanwhile, so you are likely to be considerably better off as a result.

■ You can leave your pension in the fund, as described above, and additionally contribute to a personal or stakeholder pension, provided your contributions do not exceed the (2008/09) £235,000 annual allowance.

Since April 2006, provided your scheme rules allow, you can continue working for your existing employer and draw your pension benefits, as opposed to – as previously – having to defer them until you left the organisation.

Equal pension age

Employers are required to treat men and women equally with regard to retirement and pension issues. This means that by law they must have a common retirement age that applies equally to both sexes. Similarly, they must also have a common pension age and pension schemes must offer the same benefits to their male and female members.

Divorce

Until recently, a long-standing grievance of many divorcees (ex-wives especially) was that the courts did not normally take pension benefits into account when deciding the financial arrangements between the couple. To help overcome these problems, a new provision known as pension sharing has now been made legally available in respect of divorce or annulment proceedings commenced on or after 1 December 2000. Although a main advantage of pension sharing is that it allows a clean break on divorce, many experts believe that it may well have the effect of so diminishing the husband's (or wife's) retirement fund that he (or she) may not have sufficient left to rebuild an adequate pension. Although women usually benefit most from pension sharing, the legislation equally allows an ex-husband to have a share in his former wife's pension rights.

If sadly you are in the throes of a divorce, the question of pension sharing could be a subject to raise with your solicitor. But however much in favour he/she may be, in the final analysis it is up to the court to decide on what they see as the fairest arrangement – and pension sharing is only one of the several options available to them.

Divorced wives

If you have a full basic pension in your own right, this will not be affected by divorce. However, if, as applies to many women, despite having worked for a good number of years you have made insufficient contributions to qualify for a full pension, you should contact your pension centre, quoting your pension number and NI number. It is possible that you may be able to obtain the full single person's pension, based on your ex-husband's contributions.

Your right to use your ex-husband's contributions to improve or provide you with a pension depends on your age and/or whether you remarry before the age of 60. As a general rule, you can use your ex-husband's contributions towards your pension for the years you were married (ie until the date of the decree absolute). After that, you are expected to pay your own contributions until you are 60, unless you remarry.

If you are over 60 when you divorce, then whether you remarry or not, you can rely on your ex-husband's contributions. If you remarry before the age of 60, then you cease absolutely being dependent on your former husband and instead your pension will be based on your new husband's contribution record.

NB. The same rules apply in reverse. Although it happens less frequently, a divorced man can rely on his former wife's contribution record during the years they were married to improve his basic pension. A divorced wife might have some claim to her former husband's occupational pension benefits. See section above headed 'Divorce', and also 'Pension sharing' below.

Pension sharing. As previously mentioned, provisions to enable the court to share occupational/personal pension rights at the time of divorce or annulment came into law on 1 December 2000. The legislation now equally applies to the additional State Pension. Sharing, however, is only one option for dealing with pension rights and would not necessarily apply in all cases.

Separated wives

Even if you have not lived together for several years, from a NI point of view you are still considered to be married. The normal pension rules apply including, of course, the fact that, if you have to depend on your husband's contributions, you will not be able to get a pension until he is both 65 and in receipt of his own pension. If you are not entitled to a State pension in your own right, you will receive the dependant's rate of benefit, which is about 60 per cent of the full rate (or less if your husband is not entitled to a full pension). In such a case, you can apply for income support to top up your income. Once you are 60, you can personally draw the wife's pension of £54.35 a week, without reference to your husband.

If you are under 60 but your husband has reached 65 and is retired, he may be able to claim the ADI (Adult Dependency Increase) addition of £54.35 for you. This is provided he pays it to you or is maintaining you to an equivalent amount. He will not be able to claim dependency addition if you are earning more than £60.50 a week. If your husband dies, you may be entitled to bereavement benefits in the same way as other widows. If there is a possibility that he may have died but that you have not been informed, you can check by contacting the **General Register Office** on Tel: 0845 603 7788; e-mail: gro.communications@ons.gsi.gov. uk; website: www.gro.gov.uk. As from 2008, the indexes to all birth, marriage and death entries in England and Wales will be available at the **National Archives**: Tel: 0208 876 3444; website: www.nationalarchives.gov.uk.

Widows

There are three important benefits to which widows may be entitled: bereavement benefit, bereavement allowance and widowed parent's allowance. All are largely modelled on the former widows' benefits (widow's payment, widow's pension, widowed mother's allowance), with the important difference that all are now also applicable to widowed men. To claim the benefits, fill in Form BB1, obtainable from any social security or Jobcentre Plus office. You will also be given a questionnaire (BD8) by the registrar. It is important that you complete this, as it acts as a trigger to help speed up payment of your benefits. **NB:** Widows who were already in receipt of the widow's pension before it was replaced by the bereavement allowance in April 2001 are not affected by the change and will continue to receive their pension as normal.

Bereavement benefit. This has replaced what used to be known as widow's payment. It is a tax-free lump sum of £2,000, paid as soon as a woman (man) is widowed provided that: 1) her husband had paid sufficient NI contributions; 2) she is under State retirement age; or 3) if she is over 60, her husband had not been entitled to a retirement pension. Her claim will not be affected if she is already receiving a State pension, provided this is based on her own contributions. (In the case of a widower, the male State retirement age (65) applies and receipt is dependent on his wife's NI contributions.)

Bereavement allowance. This has replaced the widow's pension. Bereavement allowance is for those aged between 45 and State pension age who do not receive widowed parent's allowance. It is payable for 52 weeks and, as with the widow's pension before, there are various levels of payment: the full-rate and the age-related bereavement allowance. Receipt in all cases is dependent on sufficient NI contributions having been paid. The full-rate bereavement allowance is paid to widows (also widowers) between the ages of 55 and 59 inclusive. The weekly amount is £90.70, which is the same as the current pension for a single person. The age-related bereavement allowance is for younger widows/widowers, who do not qualify for the full rate. It is payable to widowed persons who are aged between 45 and 54 inclusive when their partner dies. Rates depend on age and vary from £27.21 for 45-year-olds to £84.35 for those aged 54.

Bereavement allowance is normally paid automatically once you have sent off your completed form BB1, so if for any reason you do not receive it you should enquire at your social security or Jobcentre Plus office. In the event of your being ineligible, due to insufficient NI contributions having been paid, you may still be entitled to receive income support, housing benefit or a grant or loan from the social fund. Your social security or Jobcentre Plus office will advise you. As applies to the widow's pension, widows who remarry, or live with a man as his wife, cease to receive bereavement allowance.

Widowed parent's allowance. This is paid to widowed parents with at least one child for whom they receive child benefit. The current value (2008/09) is £90.70 a week. The allowance is usually paid automatically. If for some reason, although eligible, you do not receive the money, you should inform your social security or Jobcentre Plus office.

Retirement pension. Once a widow reaches 60, she would normally receive a State pension based on her own and/or her late husband's contributions. If at the time of death the couple were already receiving the State retirement pension, the widow will continue to receive her share. An important point to remember is that a widow may be able to use her late husband's NI contributions to boost the amount she receives.

Other important points. Separate from the basic pension, a widow may also receive money from her late husband's occupational pension, whether contracted in or out of the State scheme. She may also get half of any of his graduated pension.

War widows and widowers. Until recently war widows who remarried or cohabited lost their war widow's pension, unless either the cohabitation ceased or they became single again as a result of the death of their new husband, divorce or legal separation, in which circumstances their war widow's pension was restored. After years of campaigning by many groups, at last the rules have been changed and war widows can now keep their pension for life. The new rules also include men, and war widowers equally can keep a late spouse's pension for life.

Part-timers

Thanks in large part to the sex discrimination legislation being extended to include access to pension schemes, many part-timers who were previously excluded can now join their employer's occupational pension scheme as of right – or may even be able to claim retrospective membership for the years they were 'unlawfully excluded'. Their claim can only be backdated to 1976 or, if later, to the start date of their employment and must be made (at absolute latest) within six months of their leaving their job.

Part-timers who wish to claim must apply to an Employment Tribunal and, as a condition of receiving any backdated benefits due, must pay contributions in respect of those years. Although it is perhaps stating the obvious, successful appeals are not automatic, as the issue will be judged solely on grounds of sex-discrimination (and not on exclusion for other reasons).

Pensions for women

Women who have worked all their adult lives and paid full Class 1 NI contributions should get a full basic State Pension in their own right at the age of 60. The current amount is £90.70 a week; this rises every April.

Women who have only worked for part of their adult lives may not have paid enough NI contributions to get a full basic State pension on their own record. Instead, they may receive a reduced pension or one based on their husband's contributions, or one topping up the other. A wife entitled to a reduced pension on her own contributions can claim it at 60, regardless of whether or not her husband is receiving his pension.

Married women who have never worked are also entitled to a pension based on their husband's NI contributions. In money terms, the value is about 60 per cent of the level of the basic pension to which their husband is entitled. There are several important conditions, however. First, women can only receive a pension based on their husband's contributions if he himself is in receipt of a basic pension. He will have to have reached 65 and must have retired. Additionally, the wife herself must be over 60 to qualify.

If she is still under 60 when her husband claims his State pension and does not work or her earnings do not exceed £60.50, he should be able to obtain a supplement called ADI. This stands for Adult Dependency Increase, and is linked to the lowest level of the jobseekers' allowance. At present this is £54.35, which will be added to his pension on the grounds of having a wife to support. Check with the

Pensions Service on Tel: 0845 60 60 265; website: www.the
pensionservice.gov.uk.

**In contrast, if a wife has had her 60th birthday but her
husband has not yet reached 65** (or has decided to defer his
retirement), she must wait until her husband retires to
receive her share of the married couple's pension. An important point to note is that since the introduction of independent taxation, a married woman is entitled to have her
section of the joint pension offset against her own personal
allowance instead of it being counted as part of her
husband's taxable income. For many pensioner couples, this
should have the happy result of reducing their tax liability.

**If a wife who formerly worked is over 60 and retired but
cannot yet get a basic pension on either her own or her
husband's NI contributions,** she may be able to qualify for
an additional or graduated pension based on her own contributions. These are described a little further on. But first a
word about two other important matters: reduced-rate
contributions and Home Responsibilities Protection.

Reduced-rate contribution

Many women retiring today have paid a reduced rate of NI
contribution, also known as 'the small stamp'. This option
was given to working wives in 1948 and withdrawn in
1978, but women who had already chosen to pay the
reduced rate were allowed to continue, provided they did
not take more than a two-year break from employment after
1978. If you have never paid anything but reduced-rate

contributions, you are not entitled to a basic pension in your own right but instead must rely on your husband's contributions for the married couple's pension.

Home Responsibilities Protection (HRP)

Men and women, whether single or married, who have been unable to work regularly because they have had to stay at home to care for children and/or a disabled or elderly person may be able to safeguard their pension by claiming Home Responsibilities Protection. This is a very important benefit, especially for the many single women in their 50s who are sacrificing their career to look after an elderly parent. This measure was introduced in 1978 and protection only applies therefore from this date. The person you are caring for must come into one of the following categories:

▦ a child under 16 for whom you are getting child benefit;

▦ someone who you are looking after regularly for at least 35 hours a week, who is in receipt of attendance allowance, constant attendance allowance or disability living allowance;

▦ someone – for example, an elderly person – for whom you have been caring at home and in consequence have been getting income support (or supplementary benefit in the past);

▦ a combination of the above situations.

A married woman or widow cannot get HRP for any tax year in which she was only liable to pay reduced-rate NI contributions. HRP can only be given for complete tax years (6 April to 5 April), so if you simply gave up work for a few weeks in order to help out, you would be unlikely to qualify. Additionally, HRP cannot be used to reduce your total working life to below 20 years. To obtain a claim form, you should ask your pension centre for leaflet CF411.

Since 1978, anyone in receipt of child benefit, supplementary benefit or income support who is caring for someone in one of the eligible categories listed above is automatically credited with HRP. All other claimants should obtain leaflet CF411 from their pension centre.

There are concerns that up to 500,000 women over the age of 60 may be losing out on more than £1 billion in State pension entitlement through not receiving HRP. Because the HRP system reduces the number of qualifying years to receive a full State pension for women who have taken time off work to bring up children, this benefit should have been given automatically to women who were not working and receiving child benefit at any time after April 1978, when the system was introduced. Thousands of women are unaware of this and are not receiving full pensions because the government's system has failed to automatically adjust their qualifying pension years.

To get clarification, any woman over 60 or within four months of retirement should contact the Pension Service on Tel: 0845 60 60 265 or 0845 3000 168 (www.thepension service.gov.uk) to find out whether her State pension is calculated with the benefit of HRP.

Graduated pension

This scheme operated between April 1961 and April 1975. Anyone earning over £9 a week and over age 18 at the time would probably have paid graduated NI contributions and be due a pension. You can only get a graduated pension based on your own personal contributions. However, the pension from the graduated scheme is likely to be small. Further, women were penalised because their pension was calculated at a less favourable rate than for men on account of their longer life expectancy.

Additional pension

The additional State Pension scheme started with SERPS in 1978. As mentioned earlier, SERPS was discontinued by the government in April 2002 and has been replaced by a similar scheme called the State Second Pension (S2P). Women in contracted-out pension schemes are entitled either to a pension that is broadly equal to or better than its State equivalent, or to what are known as protected rights (ie their and their employer's compulsory contributions together with their accumulated investment growth).

Useful reading

Pensions for Women – Your guide (PM6) and *State Pensions for Parents and Carers – Your guide* (PM9), obtainable from the Pensions Info-Line on Tel: 0845 731 3233; website: www.thepensionservice.gov.uk.

Retiring Soon – What you need to do about your pension, free booklet available from the FSA. Tel: 0845 606 1234; website: www.fsa.gov.uk/consumer.

Stop press

Pension funds

The ceiling on tax relief given to people with pension funds up to £1.8 million will be maintained until 2015–2016.

Help for pensioners

The Pension Credit, which is the minimum income guaranteed to pensioners on modest incomes, will be increased in April 2009 from £124.05 to £130.00 a week for individuals and from £189.35 to £198.45 for couples.

The basic State Pension for a single person rises from £90.70 to £95.25 and from £145.05 to £152.30 for a couple. But this had been announced previously and has not been changed.

Pension and child benefit increases take effect in January 2009, three months early.

From January 2009 every pensioner also receives a £60 one-off payment, rising to £120 for couples, on top of the £10 bonus, to help pay for energy bills.

Summary

Hopefully, the foregoing has given you food for thought about your future, your finances and retirement planning. Each individual will have different ideas and needs as to what should be done prior to, or upon taking, retirement. However, the information above is fairly comprehensive. You may not have the time (or inclination) to deal with it all at once. However, certain things should not be left. If you think there might be a problem or you are in doubt about a particular area, it is sensible to seek professional advice and sort things out as soon as possible. Forewarned is forearmed and a problem never got better by being ignored.

If you are prepared to keep an eye on the figures, you should be well set to enjoy a long and happy retirement.

Notes

110 ▓ Notes

ALSO AVAILABLE FROM KOGAN PAGE

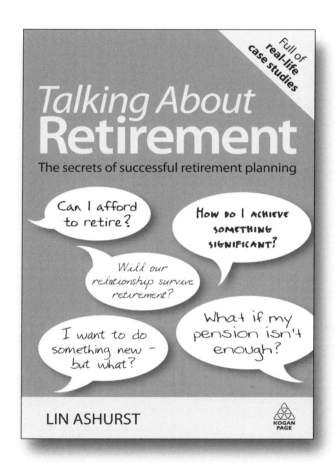

ISBN: 978 0 7494 5515 6   Paperback   2009

ALSO AVAILABLE FROM KOGAN PAGE

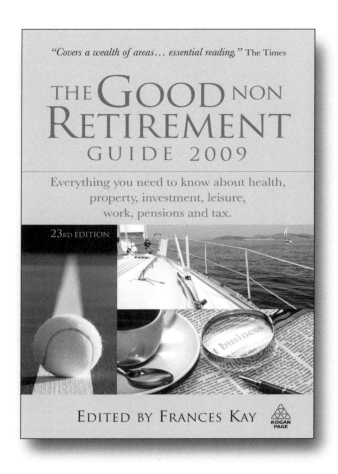

"Covers a wealth of areas... essential reading." The Times

THE GOOD NON RETIREMENT GUIDE 2009

GUIDE 2009

Everything you need to know about health, property, investment, leisure, work, pensions and tax.

23RD EDITION

EDITED BY FRANCES KAY

KOGAN PAGE

ISBN: 978 0 7494 5272 8   Paperback   2009